APPS

App Design and App Development Made Simple

Contents

Introduction

Mobile app development is now one of the biggest industries in the world ($35 billion and still growing). While it is a relatively easy field to enter, things can still get overwhelming for beginners. They will have a lot of questions and maybe some negative thoughts. Also, like in any field, not all aspiring mobile app developers succeed. Most failures happen during the first stage. Thus, this book is written to help aspiring app developers avoid those circumstances.

This book contains proven steps and strategies on how you can create your first app and profit from it. This book showcases kicking off with your app idea, the hardware and software you'll need for app development, decisions to make, preparation, app design, and how to make your app discoverable.

Thanks again for downloading this book, I hope you enjoy it!

CHAPTER 1

An Overview of Mobile App Development

Mobile apps have become really popular nowadays and, like many things, popularity translates into profit. Smartphone and tablet sales rise continuously. More than 700,000 apps are on the Play Store (Android) and App Store (iOS) today. That's not counting apps for Windows phones. By 2015, mobile app development is estimated to become a $35 billion industry. It won't be surprising if you want to cash in on this; that would actually be a smart move.

It is relatively easy to learn mobile app development yet it is also highly profitable. Many people who don't have a computer science degree are able to program apps in their free time and earn a good deal from it.

However, there are still things you need to learn in order to succeed in app development. The word "relatively" is inserted before the adjective "easy" above for a reason. Compared to programming other stuff, mobile apps are indeed easier, generally speaking. However, that doesn't mean it would be a walk in the park. Well, anyone with a computer may be able to program an app. The question is: Would it bring them considerable profits?

There are strategies you would want to follow if you want to be successful in mobile app development, but then, "success" is a subjective term. If what it means to you is "to be able to create an app," then all you need to learn is what hardware and software you need and how to use them. However, if success means "to make an app that would be popular among users and would bring me large amounts of cash" or at least "to make an app that would be in the top 100," then there is a lot more involved and deeper learning you must do. It's not just about programming your app. There are a lot of tutorials presented in various formats that you can follow and you'll be able to program in a matter of days. You won't have to enroll into some formal class to learn the necessary languages. The internet has a lot of easy-to-digest sources for that, and you might actually find that the easy part. Success in mobile app development goes beyond that. It requires creativity, a sense of design, a keen eye for the market trend, and, of course, an idea (more on this later).

Target Market

Targeting is a crucial part of any business, and if you aim to earn from your mobile app/s, you will be running a business. You will be offering something to mobile device users and they will be the ones to decide whether it's worth spending their money on your app/s or not. Each user will have different needs and wants but these can be categorized into groups for you to easily figure out your target market.

Of course, you can try to create an app that caters to everyone. Well, that would take a really useful app or a game, which appeals to all ages. People have accomplished that before. The Facebook Mobile app is an example. Almost everyone's on Facebook nowadays and most, if not all, of those who have a Facebook account would like to access it via their mobile devices. Games like Angry Birds, Candy Crush, and Flappy Bird among others have been downloaded and loved by millions of users. These apps raked in big earnings for their creators and developers. Moreover, these apps made names for their developers. Thus, users automatically consider their future apps worldwide. So, you see, a really great app not only lets you earn from its sales but also gives you a break in the mobile app industry. Your future apps will already have a guaranteed attention.

Accomplishing the above sure has great rewards. It sounds tempting, right? Indeed, it is. However, it's not easy. First of all, coming up with such an app would be hard. You might be creative enough to think of something along that line, but it's likely that someone already thought of it before you did. Thus, the app already exists. It's already in the market – put up there with an already established developer. For example, everyone has a use for communication apps such as instant messengers or email. But this is such an obvious fact that there are already apps available for such functions. There is already a dominant app for it and users of that will not likely forgo it for a similar app. Can you be it? Maybe, but it would be quite hard.

On a related note, the competition is fierce on a totally different level. Your competitors are better positioned already. They've made their names already. They have stronger means of marketing. They already have customer loyalty. Even if your app is objectively superior, the average user will easily choose theirs over yours. Worse, they might never even know your app exists. Is it possible for a beginner to trump all these challenges? Yes. The keyword is "possible." But is it likely? No.

With that, it is wiser for a beginner in mobile app development to start with a more specific target. With this, you will have to make several choices. We'll discuss these in greater detail in a later chapter.

CHAPTER 2

It All Starts with an Idea

No matter how good you are at computer programming, you won't be able to create an app without an idea. Besides, mobile app development doesn't require heavy technical knowledge of programming. You still have to learn programming languages but not at a "computer nerd" level.

So, it all starts in your head. You probably already have one since the early days of mobile apps. If you don't, there are different points where you can start off.

Check the web for some innovative function that can be ported and will also be useful for mobile use. The web and mobile apps are different but many things that work on the web are also viable as mobile apps. Examples can be easily seen. Just look at social network sites and their mobile counterparts. There are also sites that aggregate news – sorting them via keywords and more. That would be nice as an app too.

Another starting point is your own want or need. Think about an app that you searched for before but didn't find any that can match your purpose. Why not create that app yourself? Chances are, there are many other people out there who are looking for that kind of app.

Or you can think of an app that simplifies complex or tedious things. For example, uninstalling apps on a smartphone or tablet is done via numerous steps. What if you built an app that allows users to reduce that to a few taps?

If you're planning a game, your best bet would be simple yet engaging gameplay. You must also be prepared to invest in a professional graphic design talent. Originality would take you far but there's also success in building from an already existing idea. There are games out there that have similar gameplay's to some other pre-existing games but became more popular.

Well, most ideas aren't perfect right off the bat, especially when they are still in your head. Start by writing things down. Mind mapping can help. You can refine your idea at this point. However, it's likely for you to find a point of improvement along the other stages of the app development. So, don't stress yourself too much. As you go along with your app's development, you can keep refining it as you see fit.

Research is Always Valuable

Research will take you a long way in formulating and refining your app idea. Start by browsing the app list of the respective platform you chose. You may think you have a completely new idea but with hundreds of thousands of apps already in the market, creating an app with a never-before-seen function is nigh impossible. This should not discourage you, though. What you need to focus on is your own project, how it will stand out from the rest (including similar apps), and your acquirement of users. You should actually check out similar apps to give you better insight on the basic structure, main features, and what you can offer to make your app more appealing and useful to users. Take note of the key achievements as well as the mistakes made by the developers of these apps.

In the research phase, you will also gather inspiration on designing your app – from how it looks to how it works. This will let you have an easier time in several phases of the development. It will also give you ideas of what direction to take. Also, by looking at similar

APPS

apps, you will get information regarding your own app's technical requirements.

Another thing you should get from research is the marketing models for apps. You'll get insight on the best vehicles for promotion as well as effective techniques for advertising to reach the people who need your apps. You'll also see how other developers monetize your apps. Unlike your actual app idea, it's not a bad thing to imitate these things from your competitors as long as it would be effective for you.

CHAPTER 3

Choices to Make

Now, let's say you finally have your app idea. It's time to make choices. Your earliest choice would probably be the platform. Would you create an app for Android, iOS, or Windows? Of course, you can make a version of your app for each of them but it's important to have a main focus. Each one has its advantages and disadvantages but it largely just rests on your preference. If you're already a dedicated iOS fan, then no amount of comparison will convince you to develop for the other two and vice-versa.

However, if you are really giving each platform equal amounts of consideration, here are some points to think about:

The most solid in profits when it comes to app sales is the iOS. So, if earnings are your foremost priority, focus on iOS. The Play Store of Google has a higher number of apps, but the apps on the Apple App Store rake in more earnings. That's because the Android platform suffers from a high amount of piracy. There's also the problem with fragmentation. Then, Apple device users are apparently more willing to pay for apps. However, you'd need a really good capital if you plan to develop for the iOS. First off, a Mac is a must have. Second, Apple requires you to pay $99 per year. Otherwise, your app won't be in the App Store.

If your plan is to offer your app for free and just earn from ads, Android is a better choice. In general, paid apps are less frequently downloaded compared to free apps. This is actually the most recommended route for beginners. If your app gains massive popularity, you can always turn it into a paid one in the future.

If your aim is to try out new things, earning isn't that much of a concern, and if your app idea has already been adapted by lots of iOS and Android apps, then Windows 8 can be a good choice for you. It's a territory only beginning to be explored so competition is not that heavy. Windows mobile device users can discover your app/s more easily compared to the Play Store or App Store.

The platform you choose will definitely have an impact on how successful your app will be. Still, you need to remember that your app must stand out – either by having a high level of originality or offering something better than the current best apps. We'll get into what makes an app great in a later chapter.

Who will be the Users?

Like mentioned earlier, choosing your target audience is important. This will help you organize your marketing efforts. There's no sense in exerting effort in advertising your app/s to those who won't have use for it. For example, your app helps parents find and schedule educational shows for children. Thus, your marketing efforts must be directed towards parents. It will be a waste to have it seen by teens. Sure, they may find it interesting and recommend it to people in your target market. However, it is more likely for them to ignore it.

Demographics aren't the sole basis of classifying mobile app users. You must also consider varying personalities and preferences. Sometimes, people may choose one app over another solely based on its color scheme. While that may not become that big of an issue, it is still a good pointer to keep in mind.

Your target audience doesn't only direct your marketing efforts. For example, your app's interface must be appropriate for the age of the people who will use it. If it's for elder people or children, then your fonts must be generally big so they can read it easily. As another example, answer this question: would your app be mainly for smartphone users or tablet users? There is an important element here called "screen real estate" – tablets will have larger screens, which mean there is more freedom in the design. You can put more elements without making the app look crowded. We'll talk more about design later.

Figuring out your target audience won't be difficult in most cases; your app will probably determine that for you. Also, by choosing a platform, you already chose your audience to a certain extent. While each user is different, people who prefer a certain platform share similar characteristics. That influences how useful your app will appear to be.

Two Types of Apps

Another choice for you: would you build a native app or a web app? When people talk about apps, they are generally referring to native apps. These are apps that are installed on the device. On the other hand, mobile web apps are those that are accessed through the device's web browser.

Native apps are platform dependent – each one works only on its corresponding platform. Web apps are platform independent. Whichever platform the device has, it can access the app as long as it has a web browser. If you create a web app, anyone who has a smartphone or tablet can access it without the need for you to create a separate version for each platform. You can brush aside the pointers for platform choice above.

Thus, web apps are inherently more versatile, but how often have you heard about a popular web app? Most people don't even know there are such things. The point of this book, as you might already found obvious, is to guide you in building native apps. This section is just here to let you know that there is such a distinction.

The above are just the major choices you'll be making. As you develop your app, you'll be making more decisions that will be specific to your app. In the next chapter, you'll learn about the preparations to make for mobile app development.

CHAPTER 4

What Do You Need?

To create your app, you have to put it from your head (or notes) on the computer. There are preparations to make for you to be able to do that.

A Powerful Computer

First off, let's talk about the hardware. You need to have a high-end computer. It's true that you can program an app with a decent enough computer – many development kits are usable even if your computer is not that powerful. But with a powerful computer, you can test your apps more efficiently. Thus, you reduce the risk of disappointing users who download your apps because of bugs and other issues.

A high-end computer is particularly crucial for developing Android apps. That's because Android emulators have relatively heavier requirements. You need a fast processor and a large RAM to run those emulators. If you use a weak computer, the emulators will run slowly, if you are able to run them at all. You'll be wasting time on slow-downs and crashes.

A PC would be enough for developing apps for Android and Windows. It's important to get it to run Windows 8 OS if you'll be programming Windows mobile apps. On the other hand, programming iOS apps will require you to have a Mac. The best development tools for iOS mobile apps are only available on the OS X. As of today, there's no viable equivalent for the PC. At bare minimum, you need to have an Intel-based Mac running on Snow

Leopard but Mountain Lion is better. You can start with a Mac Mini. If you want to take it to the next level, then iMac is the best choice for a desktop solution. If you want a portable solution, then the MacBook Air and MacBook Pro are good choices.

Having a large display is not necessarily a requirement for you to create well-functioning apps. An 11-inch screen should suffice. However, large screens do give you advantages in your development process. Many development tools are faster and more convenient to use with a larger screen size. A multiple-monitor setup seems luxurious but if you can afford it, by all means go for it.

An Actual Device

In developing apps, you'll need to have mobile devices corresponding to your chosen platform. Chances are you already have a smartphone so this would be quite easy. However, some experts recommend having a separate device for development apart from that for your personal uses. This will be costly, especially if you are developing for iOS devices, but it would be a good investment. Since you're a beginner, especially if you have a tight budget, it's okay if you don't have a separate device for development. Just keep the following guidelines in mind:

Make sure your device matches that of your targeted market. It can be as simple as this: if you're creating an app for smartphones, your device must be a smartphone; if your app is for tablets, use a tablet.

Choosing the type of device is just the first step. There are still more things to think about. Your device must have decent specs – processing power, RAM, screen size, battery life, etc.

Make sure your device has the latest possible updates for its OS. Making your app compatible with outdated mobile software might seem a good move so that users who don't update their devices can use your apps. However, giving yourself unnecessary limitations will do more harm than good in the long run.

The mobile device will act as your very own beta tester. You might be thinking, "Why is this required if the development tools already provide emulators to test my app?" Well, emulators are yet to run exactly like the devices. The emulators are there to test for bugs. The actual user experience can only be tested on the actual device. You can see better see how the app works on a touchscreen. Moreover, there are some other issues that may only become apparent when you are testing the app on the actual device.

Software

Next is the software. Each platform would have a different set of tools for development. In order to create apps, you have to download the corresponding Software Developer Kits (SDKs) for the respective platform. There are different SDKs for each device. So, you would have to download SDKs based on the platform and your target device.

For the iOS platform, you'll need iOS x.0 SDK – where 'x' is the app's iOS version. You also need XCode, an IDE tool used in the development of iOS apps. You can download XCode from Apple's official site.

For Android, you need to download Eclipse together with the SDK you need. The recommended is Android v3.0 as it is the one compatible with the most number of Android devices. However, if you want the ability to use the advanced features of the API, download the newest SDK version – Android 4.0. You can also integrate currently existing services from Google into your app alongside the SDK. The IDE for Android apps includes the Code Editor, Interface Designer, Emulator, and Debugger.

For Windows, you'll need the Microsoft Visual Studio 2012

with an integrated SDK for your app. All the SDKs and tools are downloadable from the official Windows phone site.

Registration

To download the official tools and publish apps in their respective market, you first need to register. For iOS, you register with Apple's developer site. Upon agreeing to the terms and conditions, you will become an official Apple developer. The username and password you registered will also be your credentials for logging into iTunes. The registration is free of charge. You only need to pay the aforementioned $99 per year once you want to publish your app in the App Store.

Google has the same manner of registration – you create an account and agree to the terms and conditions. You will then be an official Google developer. To publish apps on the Play Store, you need to pay $25 per year.

Registration for Windows is via the official Windows Phone developer site. Registration is free. Once you want to publish your app on the Windows Market Place, you need to pay $49 per year.

Once you are registered to the respective platforms, you will have access to the tools you'll need in developing your own app. These include templates, code examples, tutorial videos, developer libraries, simulators for testing, interface design samples, and a lot more.

Programming Knowledge

You won't need to have a computer science (or any related) degree to become a developer. There are also web-based interfaces out there that will allow you to create apps without knowing how to write codes. You'll just need to click and drag.

However, many experts would still recommend learning programming languages. The ability to code opens up more capabilities for your app. There is no need to worry because you don't have to enroll into a school to learn them. They can be self-taught and you can learn them while developing your app.

If you already have a background in programming, developing apps won't be too difficult for you. If you don't, that's okay but it is advisable to review concepts of object-oriented programming before learning the languages.

The programming languages for the different platforms are as follows:

- iOS

- Objective-C

- SWIFT

- Android

- JAVA (for coding)

- XML (for interface design)

- Windows

- C# (for coding)

- CSS3, HTML5, or XAML scripts (for interface design)

You can find tons of sources over the internet for each of these languages. There are dedicated websites and free eBooks.

When you've prepared your hardware, software, and yourself, it's time to start creating your app. The SDKs and other tools you downloaded will have manuals (online and otherwise) which you can refer to so you know how to use them. With that, we will not discuss how to use each of them. In the next chapter, we will talk about the design of your app.

CHAPTER 5

Don't Overlook the Design

Steve Jobs gave high regard to the importance of design, and for good reason. This applies to mobile app development as well. It is one of the most crucial parts of developing your app. There are lots of apps in the markets and lots of them fail. The top reason for failure is poor design. In other words, neglecting the design aspect of your app will greatly reduce its chances of success.

Consider this: you have two apps with the same price, functionalities and extra features. However, one doesn't have a consistent look and the other has a sleek design. Which one do you think more users will choose? Of course, it will be the one with the good design. Even in the case that the latter is slightly inferior with its features, more users will choose it than the former.

The design is not only how the app looks, but also how it feels. You have to remember, the interface is how your users will interact with your app. You might have advanced functionalities in your code but the user can't use them effectively if the interface is not designed well.

The different platforms may have different presentations and methods for their apps. However, their design principles have a common root: usability. If an app isn't usable (or playable, in the case of games), then it won't succeed. You won't be the one to decide if it's usable. Of course you believe it's usable. It's what the users will believe that you have to be concerned about. The app should speak for itself and you can accomplish this with good design.

You can heighten the level of usability of the app with a good user interface. Use color contrast to make differing elements discernible. Give it intuitive controls. Don't overcrowd the screens. Choose colors that are easy on the eyes. Don't use fancy fonts. These are just few of the things you can do to increase your apps usability.

Well, the artistry of your app overall and its user interface rests only upon your own sense of creativity. There is no one advice that works for all. However, there are guidelines you can follow.

Designing iOS Apps

In designing apps for iOS, Apple has custom templates readily available for official developers. Note though that these templates are only for non-game apps. The templates will help you turn your prototype to an actual app quickly and easily. They also help towards making your app's look and feel consistent.

Using templates may be convenient but it's still a good practice to code from scratch. In this case, it's best to consult the style guide available from iTunes Connect. It can give you substantial inspiration. Moreover, conforming to this style guide actually raises your app's chances of being approved by Apple and featured in the App Store's categories.

Designing Android Apps

In the case of Android, there is a webpage over at the platform's developer site dedicated to app design. It contains all you'll ever need to know about what elements to include and principles of app design. The Android developer community develops it. If you're really stuck, then there's no better point of reference.

Aside from that page, Google put up the Android design pack on the public domain. It includes materials you can use in designing your app – color swatches, sources, icon packs, stencils, etc. With this, you can save time and effort. After all, there's really no point in creating these yourself. All you need to do is download the design pack.

Designing Windows Apps

Windows Mobile is some new ground. So, you probably won't find as many readily usable templates for it. A design guide, however, is laid out on the Windows developer site. Summarizing it here wouldn't do it justice. So, if you'll be creating apps for Windows, give that guide a good read.

Bottom Line: It Rests Upon You

If we discuss the design aspect with more depth, we can come up with a separate book. However, all the lessons will just be theories. You'll enhance your sense of design by doing it yourself.

In the next chapter, we'll look at what comes after the creation of your app: how to expose it to the users.

Top 10 Mistakes People Make when Designing and Developing Mobile Apps

Before we leave the subject of mobile app designing behind, I just want to touch on basic mistakes that people make when they are mid design. App designing is not easy – each one has a multitude of different bits to it and you have to take project management into account as well. Developing an app that both works and is fully functional takes skill, practicality and discipline. The following are the top 10 mistakes that app designers make:

1. Always Have A Flow Map

It is important that, before you begin to design your app, you have a well thought out flow map ready. This will make sure you have a logical navigational structure to go follow. Also make sure that your key functional screens are near the top; not buried underneath huge piles of navigational elements.

2. Don't Build For Multiple Platforms

At least not right away. Back in 2012, Google announced that they had as any apps in their app store as Apple did in theirs, showing just how tough the app market has truly become. Keep your costs down and concentrate on one platform at a time because this will make sure that you get your app into your chosen store as quickly as possible. Once it's out and you can judge how it goes, then you can think about building for another platform.

If you do choose to develop for two or three different platforms, consider this – when you have to make a design or function change, you have to do it on every platform. That takes time and costs more money.

3. Don't ask Your Users To Register Unless You Have Something to Offer Them

You should always allow users a period of time in which to try out your app before you ask them to sign up. Ask yourself one question – if this was a web app, would you be forcing people to sign up before allowing them access? Your app has to be of some value to a user before they are going to want to register and give you their personal details. It has to be an app that users can engage with; registration must be a natural process, not something that you force on potential customers.

4. Not Giving User Onboarding Enough Significance

User onboarding is also known as organizational socialization and is one of the hardest parts of the design process. Many designers under-estimate how skillful their users are, also their knowledge and their behavior. Onboarding is one of the single most significant aspects of designing the user experience and it is vital that you are constantly on the watch for feedback. Use built in app analytics to answer your questions – what is it about your app makes people like it? Why do they delete it?

This kind of feedback is priceless to a developer and designer and can help you to make your app one of the best there is.

5. Not Putting User Experience First When You Design Your App

User experience is the single most important part of your app design. There are a lot of developers who attempt to replicate a web design onto a mobile design and it simply doesn't work. During your design, you must put yourself in the place of a mobile user and rethink your entire strategy for interaction on a mobile app.

Also, take your time. Some people go ahead and speed through their development, releasing an app that really isn't fit for purposes and mobile app reviewers can be downright harsh. Your ratings may be in the toilet before you even get started.

Keep in mind that there are more than 1.5 million apps on the market and users have very high expectations. An app for a smartphone has be easy to find and it has to be productive. Mobile app users will very quickly pass your app over if the user experience is not intuitive enough.

6. No Consistency in the Design

It's the same thing as using 50 different words to say one thing. Some designers mix and match their design to the extent that it is a mess. You don't need to use so many different buttons or words for the same function and you shouldn't use the same command for differing actions in various parts of your app. That's the quickest way to make the user feel like screaming and kicking your app into touch. Really, there is nothing worse than using an app that leaves you wondering which direction you are going in.

If app navigation is confusing or difficult or just plain cumbersome, a user will soon lose interest. A curious user may decide to take a little time to try and untangle the web but not for long. Keep things simple – use common buttons and icons where a user would expect them to be and, if needed, use a text button.

7. Overloading Your App With Too Many Features

Developers and designers who are new to mobile apps sometimes have a tendency to put too many features into their very first app. What you should do is think hard about specific features that your users would want and concentrate on those – others can be added in later on. Many of the more popular apps are built on the solid grounding of less being more. While you might like your app to be stuffed full of features that a user may want to use one day, it isn't a good idea and it will take up an awful lot of memory and resources – your users won't be impressed with that!

If your mobile app is a companion app to a web-based one, you can tailor some of the features. The idea behind mobile apps is to make things simple and cut the functionality down to the core uses.

8. Using animations for Your Intro

While it may be nice to have the odd animation, too many of them can seriously affect the performance of your app. In technical terms, animations generally start after your app has loaded so all this is doing is holding up the user from actually using the app – that doesn't please them. If you must use animations, make them quick and make them appealing.

9. Doing Their Own Beta Testing

This is a big no-no. As the developer, you cannot possibly put yourself in an objective frame of mind. Consider allowing a select group of users to access your app and test it for you, and will give you the feedback you need. And when you get that feedback, make sure you act on it.

10. Not Making the Hit Area Big Enough

When you are designing and developing your app, it is important that you remember most users have an index finger width of 1.6-2cm wide. Users do not like finding that they struggle to hit the buttons because they are too small, or that they hit several at once. Place the buttons sufficient space apart and make sure they are big enough.

CHAPTER 6

Make it Be Seen, Make it Be Heard

So, now you've created an awesome app. It is well designed and offers a useful function. The next thing to do is to get them to the users.

A Quick Aside

We have brushed on testing previously. Its importance can never be understated. You have to make sure your app is working properly. Test it on the simulator/emulator. Then, test it on your device. If you can borrow a device (different from yours but still targeted by your app) from a friend for testing, that would be good. You'll be able to test your app on multiple devices.

App Submission

Okay, so you finished your app. Its time to put it up on the market. First you have to submit it for approval and pay the corresponding fees. Go to your respective developer account and click the corresponding "Submit App" button. Be warned: this make take a while (up to weeks). Don't be discouraged though. This is necessary. The respective app market will scan it for malicious code and evaluate your app for utility. Once your app is approved, it will be on the Play Store/App Store/Market Place.

Discoverability

Your app won't earn you a lot if you just let it sit there. Fortunately, there are things you can do to increase its discoverability and, as a result, its marketability.

Never Game the Rankings

Whatever you do, don't try to fool the rankings. If you consult people how to do so, the best they can give you are speculations. The app markets don't reveal their ranking system completely. That's only natural, as people will try to exploit the system, which would only cause dissatisfaction to the users. That would be bad for everyone – developers, hosts, and users alike. Apple, Google, and Microsoft are making efforts to prevent exploitation and it won't be wise to swim against that tide.

Keywords, Keywords...

When people look for specific apps that they need, they will more likely search for it rather than browse the lists one by one. Thus, your app will benefit if you optimize it for keywords. As much as possible, your app name must have the main keyword. If all the good names are already taken, don't fret as you can attach keywords to your app when you publish it. Relevance is highly important. Below are some guidelines on keyword choice:

Put yourself in the position of a user. What terms will you type when searching for an app similar to yours? You don't have to think them all yourself. Ask around and you'll come up with a list of relevant search terms.

Put them in order according to relevance.

You won't need to repeat keywords that are already included in your app's name or its main category.

Search functions in app markets are not as advanced as search engines. They don't account for misspellings, synonyms, and/or plurality.

Markets would have limits in the number of characters for keywords. Spaces and special characters count so separate

APPS

your keywords with spaces or commas but not both. Also, if the keywords you listed won't all fit, forgo those that have the lowest relevance and search volumes.

Utilize the Description

Once your app is optimized for keywords, it will appear in searches of people who need/want it. People will preview an app before they download it and they will see your app's description. The key here is to keep it short and simple. There is a character limit here as well. As much as possible, showcase your app's function in the first sentence (previews usually only show the first three lines) or make it interesting so that users will be attracted to read the full description.

Specify the Category

Users also search for apps by browsing by category. So, don't forget to specify the right category. Your app may have two applicable categories and it would be wise to include them both. Remember though, that the markets will list one as a primary category and the other as secondary. The primary would be used for listing and the secondary would be a support for searches. So, specify which is which when documenting your app.

Listen to Users

Pay attention to user feedback, particularly about areas of improvement and bugs. Include the fixes in the next update and make it as soon as possible. This will help your app maintain a good rating.

Offer a Free Version

Offer a "free" version of your app. Most users want to try new apps first before they pay for them. This will improve the exposure of your app.

Strategic Price Lowering

Price lowering will make your app appear more valuable when done right. Look at physical stores: when an item is on "sale" with its new lower price indicated alongside its former price (with a strikethrough), people are compelled to buy it. It also works for the app markets.

Encourage Reviews from Users

Incorporate a prompt for encouraging user reviews. People love to express their opinions, so encourage them to review your app descriptively. Whether the review is good or bad, you will get substantial insight for your next update.

Use Social Media

Incorporate a one-touch button for posting about your app on their social media. Create a fan page for your app. It's a good way of advertising.

Paid Advertising Can Pay Off

Don't shun paid advertising right away. Qualified downloads is quite effective. A qualified download is when a user downloads your app through an ad.

Take it Online

Numerous online methods can be used to promote your app. Here are just a few: Have your app reviewed by prominent bloggers in exchange for a free download of your app. Submit your app to application directories and aggregator sites.

CHAPTER 7

How Much Does it Cost to Make an App

In the last few years, the mobile app market has exploded beyond all expectations, growing by 76% in 2014 alone. The average customer in the US downloads an average of 8.8 apps per month, both iOS and Android. Now that Apple has introduced Apple Pay, the Cupertino giants have access to around 90% of credit cards in the US and that is set to grow as the feature is introduced across other countries.

There is a good reason why mobile apps have suddenly gone crazy. Having one for your business or as a promotion tool can be a real game changer and can help drive traffic and revenue your way. On the top end of the spectrum, you have the likes of Rovio, makers of Angry Birds, worth more than a billion dollars just from that one simple game. Then you have the other end of the spectrum where people put out free apps ad still generate thousands of downloads. There are those who avoid mobile apps for their businesses because they believe that they are expensive to make.

App Development Costs

Building an app is a bit like building a house. You cannot possibly answer a question on cost until you know more details and the same goes with an app. The cost of building your app is going to depend on a number of factors, including how many features it has, what they do, how the app looks and feels. The following are all things to consider when you are thinking about building an app:

Hiring the Right Developer

Software developers don't come cheap and can charge anywhere from $300 per day for a freelancer up to $1000 for a fully established company. However, the cheaper they are the less likely they are to have any real experience. Cheaper developers may take longer to produce your app and may provide you with work that needs to be redone. On the other side of the coin, the most expensive developers have the experience but they also have the overheads which need to be paid for and all of these make the cost of building your app seem just that little bit more expensive. For the best value, look for a developer that has a good track record and has lower overheads.

What Kind Of App Are You Developing?

Mobile apps can be broken down into 4 main groups, based on the amount of work required to develop them:

- **Simple Apps** - the basic cost for an app with only a couple of screens and one function can be from $1500 up to around $10,000. This kind of app does not store data about the app users or the previous uses for the app.

- **Database/API Apps** – Apps that require information being stored on a remote server or on the app user's device are somewhat more complex to build. If you want your users to have access to features like being able to save lists, register and log in or synch between several different devices, then you can expect to pay anywhere from $7,000 to $45,000.

- **Multi-featured/Enterprise Apps** – These apps are the central part of your business and users are able to access information on any mobile device or web browser. The app may have a number of key features and the interface is specially designed to offer a completely immersive experience. You can expect to pay upwards of $45,000 for this kind of app.

- **Games** – Probably the most popular category, games can range from dead simple up to highly complex and you can expect to pay between $10,000 and $300,000.

The Costs of Common Features

Social Media Integration – allowing users access to Twitter and Facebook from the app or using Facebook to sign into your app - $400 to $1500

In-App Purchases – Charging users for additional services and downloads from within your app - $1500 to $4500

Game Center – If you are developing a game and want to register it on the game center on iOS - $1200

How Long Will It Take To Develop?

This is another question that is not easy to answer because of everything that goes into building an app and all of the variables. A simple app could be done within a week but more complex larger apps can take up to a year.

Additional Costs to Consider

Designing and building your app are not the only costs you have to take into consideration. The following are other things you will need to facto into your cost:

Testing – The price for testing your app will depend on the complexity and the size of it. Testing is more about investing time but is one of the most important aspects of app building. If your app doesn't work properly or is full of bugs, you want to know before you put the app to market. Putting it right afterwards is often too little too late.

- $99 - iTunes Developer account. If you want your app in the iOS app store, you have to pay $99 per year.

- $150/month - Servers and back-end support. Expect to pay this if your app is reliant on a web server to store data

- +25% - Native iPad Support. If you have built an app for the iPhone and want to add in support for the iPad as well. This will take more design and development so you can add about 25% to the total cost of building your app.

- $1500 to $4500 - Marketing. It's a complete waste of time and money building your app if no one can find it to use it. Marketing is vital when you are launching a new app and it is a cost you need to factor into the equation.

CHAPTER 8

Building Your Very First App – iOS

In 2014, Apple introduced a brand new computer programming language. It is called Swift and iOS developers can use it in place of Objective C. Because it is so new, there really isn't anyone who could call him or herself an expert just yet. Design patterns are still being found and people are writing about what it can do as they find out. That said, those that have used it are extolling its virtues over Objective C, claiming it is a much friendlier language to write in. So, we are going to look at building your first app using Swift.

What You Need

You will need:

- A Mac OS X computer running Yosemite or Mavericks

- Xcode 6

Getting Started

As soon as you have installed Xcode and you have everything set up, launch Xcode.

Press Cmd+Shift+N to create a new project

In the Template selector, check that iOS – Application is checked off

Choose the Master Detail Application template

This is a good template to start with as it already has a storyboard set up with most of what we will need, as well as having controllers for both the Master controller and the Detail controller. Why are we using this? Because we are going to create a task list app.

Once you have selected the Master Detail Application, click on Next to move on to the next section. In the next screen, you need to fill in a few options. Start by naming your app in the Product Name field. For the purposes of this tutorial, call your app TaskMe.

Next fill in your organization name and in the organization identifier field, use a reverse domain name to use in the identifier – for example, Com.airpair. The organization identifier is going to help you create your bundle identifier. This is what is used to give your application a unique name for Apple and Apple devices.

In the Language menu, make sure that Swift is selected, not Objective C. This will ensure that the code generated by Xcode will be in Swift and not in Objective C files.

Lastly, in the Devices menu, select iPhone and check that Use Core Data is not checked. While core data is good to learn about, for the purposes of this tutorial, we are just taking a look at creating an iOS application.

Part 1 - Learning by Example

Before we get into actually writing any code, let's have a look at the Swift codes that was generated for you when you chose the Master Detail Application earlier on.

This is already a working application so, to see what it does, press on Cmd+R to build and run the application

As you can see, you begin in a list screen that has an Edit and + button. Tapping + will allow you to add another row to the list.

The row will show the date and the time that the row was added. Tapping on the new row brings up a details screen, with the date and time in the center of the screen. From the list screen, either swipe and press delete to remove a row or tap on Edit and delete from in there.

Let's have a look as the Swift code generated by Xcode:

- AppDelegate.swift

The point of entry to our application will be the AppDelegate.swift file so let's begin looking at the code in there first. You will see some comments at the top of the file; ignore these. The first line of code you see should be:

- import UIKit

This is the key that opens the door to all sorts of goodies available in the UIKit in this file. If you are familiar with Objective C, then this will also be familiar to you but this time we are importing a module rather than header files for a framework or class. This is going to be done in virtually every file within your iOS application, whether it is for UIKit or for the much simpler Foundation files.

The next line of code you see is

- @UIApplicationMain

Unlike other computer languages, Swift does not contain a main file. Instead, it is up to you to tell Xcode which file should be the main one by adding in this attribute to a Swift class. The chances of you moving this from where Xcode puts it is slim to none but at least you know exactly what the code is for now.

Now we know the class definition for AppDelegate and you can see that inherits from UIResponder and the UIApplicationDelegate protocol. This is huge improvement over the way Objective-C worked:

- class AppDelegate: UIResponder, UIApplicationDelegate {

If you look through the implementation of the AppDelegate class you can see there isn't a great deal going on inside. There is one Window variable and a whole bunch of functions that are empty or mostly empty. There is just one function that has an executable code:

- application:didFinishingLaunchingWithOptions:

All that is doing is returning true:

- func application(application: UIApplication, didFinishLaunchingWithOptions launchOptions: [NSObject: AnyObject]?) -> Bool {

- // Override point for customization after application launch.

- return true

- }

In your project settings, we have the Main.storyboard file, which has been set as the launching point for the application. This will set the window and controllers up when the application launches. The only other code that is worth a mention in this file is the variable definition for Window:

- var window: UIWindow?

What this is going to do is create a variable property on AppDelegate with its type as an optional UIWindow. This is expressed as UIWindow? – note that it ends with a question mark.

If you know nothing at all about optionals, they are basically the only types that are able to hold something or be nil. One other important thing to note about optionals is the way they are used in parameter types. At the ends of some Swift types, you will see an exclamation mark – this is known as an implicitly unwrapped optional:

- @IBOutlet weak var detailDescriptionLabel: UILabel!

The difference between a normal optional and an implicitly unwrapped optional is that, if you attempt to use the implicitly unwrapped optional without a value you will get a runtime error. The same would be true if you attempted to unwrap and use a normal optional with no value. This is why these optionals are only ever used where there will always be a value.

Notice that the second parameter of

- application:didFinishLaunchingWithOptions:

has got two names. The first is

- didFinishLaunchingWithOptions

this is the public name for when the function is called and, the second name

- launchOptions

is the constant name while it is being used in the scope of the function

- func application(application: UIApplication,
  didFinishLaunchingWithOptions launchOptions:
  [NSObject: AnyObject]?) -> Bool {

MasterViewController.swift

When you open up the MasterVeiwController.Swift file, you can see straight away that this is a much busier place. You saw Import within the AppDelegate.swift file and I'm sure you have already figured out that the MasterViewController class inherits from UITableViewController. Rather than going over every piece of code, I'm just going to brush over the good parts that Swift improves on when compared to Objective C methods.

A quick look over the ode show up one thing above everything else- the use of a keyword called override in front of virtually every function:

- override func awakeFromNib() {

- override func viewDidLoad() {

- override func didReceiveMemoryWarning() {

Because most of these functions are already defined in the superclass for MasterViewController you must tell the compiler that you definitely want to override or extend the functionality that is already there in the ancestor functions. This helps cut down on errors where you might use a function name by accident when it has already been used, which would cause everything to break!

When you look at your MasterViewController class, you can see that the first part is the objects variable property definition, initialized with an NSMutableArray, which is empty:

- var objects = NSMutableArray()

When the view for your controller has finished loading, the viewDidLoad method will be called – this starts by calling the superclass method, pretty much the same as every similar function.

The superclass call is followed by setting up the bar button items on the left or the right and the interesting thing of note here is the use of a constant for the addButton function. This is a suggested method for all things that do not change after they have been created. The other interesting part is the initialization of the UIBarButtonItem:

- UIBarButtonItem(barButtonSystemItem: .Add, target: self, action: "insertNewObject:")

Instead of using verbose syntax like you do in Objective C, you simply use named arguments in the initializer. There is also a notably nicer way of telling it which UIBarButtonSystemItem you want:

- UIBarButtonSystemItem.Add

Taking a look at the insertNewObject: function, note the sending parameter of AnyObject:

- func insertNewObject(sender: AnyObject) {

We don't need to use it in this function so let's move on to tableVi ew:cellForRowAtIndexPath:

- override func tableView(tableView: UITableView, cellForRowAtIndexPath indexPath: NSIndexPath) -> UITableViewCell {

- let cell = tableView.dequeueReusableCellWithIdentifier("C ell", forIndexPath: indexPath) as UITableViewCell

- let object = objects[indexPath.row] as NSDate

- cell.textLabel?.text = object.description

- return cell

- }

On the first line, we have called dequeueReusableCellWithIdentifier:forIndexpath and the return for this is AnyObject. Any kind of class can be returned from this function call so you must type cast it using as UITableViewCell that you see on the end f the line. Later on, we will change this to the custom cell class of TaskCell that you will be creating later on.

The last part of interest is the syntax used for mark comments, helping you to split and jump through file:

- // MARK: - Table View

Using this syntax for comments allows you to split the file, which means you can jump through it, and readers can also understand better what the functions inside a file are related to.

DetailViewController.swift

This is the last of the Xcode generated files to look at and is quite a bit smaller than the MasterViewControlle file. That said, it is still full of good examples of how Swift helps us to write better code.

We start off with the @IBOutlet attribute for detailDescriptionLabel variable. In the same way as it was for Objective C header files, this attribute tells Interface Builder about the property on the DetailViewController:

- @IBOutlet weak var detailDescriptionLabel: UILabel!

This variable has also been designed to be weak because you don't want DetailViewController as the owner of the view.

Next is an interesting property definition that has a bit of extra code attached to define the behavior of a property that is next to its definition.

- var detailItem: AnyObject? {

- didSet {

- // Update the view.

- self.configureView()

- }

- }

Note the optional AnyObject type and also the didSet code block.

Properties can contain blocks of code that are executed as callbacks to specific event. The good thing about this is, instead of defining a setter to do this, you get a much clearer definition of why the code is there.

So, you can see that the code now states clearly that after the DetailItem is set, configureView should be called at any time because something that relates to the view has been changed. These callbacks are a huge leap forwards in terms of the expressive nature of coding for iOS apps.

Just quickly going back to the subject of optionals, you can see how they are used in the following piece of code:

- func configureView() {

- // Update the user interface for the detail item.

- if let detail: AnyObject = self.detailItem {

- if let label = self.detailDescriptionLabel {

- label.text = detail.description

- }

- }

- }

We are using an optional binding in an if statement – this means that the right hand side of the statement will be assigned to the left hand side of the expression ONLY if it has a value. If it doesn't have a value, the main body of the if statement will be ignored. This is similar to the way we check for a nil in Objective C but much safer and much more expressive.

Part 2 – Adding Functionality

So far, you have learned how swift works differently to Objective C and how it has an effect on the way you work with APIs and Cocoa Touch classes. It is important that you understand this because, if you start to write apps like you did in Objective C, you would soon be battling against Swift.

What we are looking at is how to make it safer to build an app without losing the expressiveness of the Swift language.

For the next step, we are going to use the TaskMe application that you generated at the beginning, using Xcode and we are going to start adding some real functionality into it.

The first thing we are going to do is add the ability to be able to add new tasks to your task list. Once you have created this feature, it will be a simple task of tapping the + button, typing in the title of your task and adding in some notes if you want. When you tap on Save, you will go back to your task list.

So, for the user interface we want to be able to allow the user to tap on a + button and bring up a new controller. To do this we need to open up Main.storyboard.

You need to use two controllers for this – a UIViewController and a UINavigationController. So, go into the object library and bring these two controllers out into the editor area – the objects library is locate at the bottom right hand side of Xcode

A table view controller will have been created with the UINavigationController – delete it and then hold CTRL, click the UINavigationController and drag it across to UIViewController. A popup will appear; select Root View Controller from the Relationship Segue section. What this will do is embed the UIViewController into the UINavigationController so that you will be able to add Save and Cancel buttons in to it later on.

The next step is to set up the segue so that you can navigate both the UIViewController and the UINavigationController but, before that, you need to open the MasterViewController.swift file, locate the viewDidLoad method and delete the following two lines:

- let addButton = UIBarButtonItem(barButtonSystemItem: .Add, target: self, action: "insertNewObject:")

- self.navigationItem.rightBarButtonItem = addButton

You can also delete the insertNewObjec: method.

Now go back to the Main.Storyboard file, open the object library and drag a Bar Button Item to the right hand side of the navigation bar in masterViewController. Open the Attributes inspector and change the identifier to Add.

Now we can set up the segue from the MasterVewController to UINavigationController. To do this, hold CTRL and drag from the

BarButton you created to the UINavigationalController. From the Action Segue menu in the popup, select Present Modally.

The new segue looks like a rectangle inside a circle, pas of an arrow that is between the UINavigationController and the MasterViewController. Locate it and select it, then use the Attributes Inspector to set the identifier to showAddTask.

All that is left to do now is set up the screen. Go to the Object Library and drag 2 Text Fields to the UIViewController. Position them how you think they should be. Try to set up Auto Layout Constraints by holding CTRL and dragging through the text fields and the containing view.

When you have selected the first text field, you need to edit a few of the settings in the Attributes Inspector. So, open the Attributes Inspector and go to the empty placeholder – change it so it says Task Title and change the size of the font to 24 points. This can be done through Font editor – open this by clicking the T icon beside the font.

Now, we want to play about with the height so you should change the border style to the second from the right. Once you've done that, you can make the text field any height you want – go for 60 points tall and change the alignment to centered.

Now repeat all of that for the second text field but give it a slightly smaller font size, maybe 16 points, make the height slightly shorted and give the placeholder text a name like Notes. Then set the alignment to the left, not the center as you did the first one.

In the UIViewController, click on the navigation bar and, in the attributes inspector, set the title to Add Task. You now have two text fields and the controllers set up for your app. Next, we will be creating the subclass for the UIViewController for the Add

Task screen. First, try running the application to check that you can actually open a new screen – you will not be able to get back though so don't worry about that at the moment.

Creating the AddTaskViewController

Open the File Menu, choose New and then File or use Cmd+N on the keyboard to start creating the AddTaskViewController file. Check that you are still in iOS>Source and then select Cocoa Touch Class from the list of options. Click on Next.

In the Subclass Of: field, input UIViewController – either type it or select it. Then add in AddTask to the start of the name in the Class field.

Check that Also Create in XIB is not checked and that Swift is chosen language. Click on Next. You will now see a file dialogue – select the file location and click on Create.

Now, a file is going to appear but, before you start to edit it, you must remember to set it to be the class for the UIViewController created in Storyboard. To do this, open Main.Storyboard and select the UIViewController; set the class to AddTaskViewController in the small panel at the top that looks like a square and lines – this is the identity inspector.

Now that the focus is on AddTaskViewController in the Interface Builder, open the Assistant Editor (it's an icon that looks like a tuxedo in the toolbar) so that we can set the outlets between the code and the Storyboard.

Hold CTRL and drag from each text field to the top of the class definition for AddTaskViewController. Name each text field titleField and notesField respectively. You should now see something like:

- class AddTaskViewController: UIViewController {

- @IBOutlet weak var titleField: UITextField!

- @IBOutlet weak var notesField: UITextField!

- override func viewDidLoad() {

@IBOutlet declares the connection between your code and the Storyboard file. It uses an implicitly unwrapped optional because the view controller doesn't need this set to be initialized, leaving it so you can set them later on when the views are ready. It won't really affect you too much because by the time you get round to setting things up viewDidLoad or viewWillAppear: animated, it will already be set by then.

Note the weak variable declaration. This is to ensure that there are no references that are not necessary. With this weak variable, AddTaskViewController would own the text fields and that would stop the view attempts from being released – the controller will be hanging on to the sub views.

Cancelling Task Creation

Ok, so now we are ready for the next step which to set the Cancel button up. Tapping on this button will hide the task creation screen without saving your work. Go into the Main.Storyboard file, drag a Bar Button item from the Objects library, and put it to the left side of the navigation bar in AddtaskViewController.

Select the item and go into Attributes Inspector, set the identifier to Cancel.

There are two reasons why you should be using the standard versions of the UI elements – one is accessibility and the other is future proofing. You could easily set the title to Cancel but let's say that Apple changes Cancel to an X in the future, your app will now be ready for that. The standard elements also have accessibility built n and have been well and truly tested by Apple developers.

The next job is to get the Cancel button hooked up and to do that we need to create a Dismiss segue. S, open the File menu, select Create a New File and, from the window that pops up, choose iOS>Source>Cocoa Touch Class. Click on Next. Set the Subclass of: toUIStoryboardsegue and set Class as DismissSegue. Ensure that Swift is selected for the language.

Before you can use this class in your Storyboard, there is one more tweak that we need to make. At the moment, it will allow a Dismiss segue to show up in Interface Builder but at runtime it will fail because of some odd naming stuff that Swift does in the background. To fix this, you have to explicitly define the Class name so that Storyboard can find the correct one. The class definition should look like this:

- @objc(DismissSegue) class DismissSegue: UIStoryboardSegue {

The declaration at the start of that class definition is designed to make it accessible for the Storyboard. This may change as time goes by but for now it is a must and the app will not run properly without it.

The next job is to create a perform method for the custom segue, that will dismiss the controller:

- override func perform() {

- if let controller = sourceViewController. presentingViewController? {

- controller.dismissViewControllerAnimated(true, completion: nil)

- }

- }

All that's left to do now is connect the dots together. Go into the Main.Storyboard file, hold CTRL and drag from the Cancel button to the MasterViewController. From the popup, select Dismiss.

Now simply run the app to see if it all works OK.

Saving Our Task

Now, it's time to get to the real business value, saving tasks, and for that you need to create a Save button. In the Main.Storyboard file, go into the Objects library, drag out yet another Bar Button Item, and place it on the right side of the navigation bar on the AddTaskViewController.

Select the item, go into Attributes Inspector and change the identifier to Save. While you are there, we need to clean up something. When people use your app, they are not going to care much that the list screen is the main Master screen; as far as they are concerned, it is a task screen so double click on Master and change it to Tasks. Now add the Dismiss segue between Save and MasterViewController in the same way you did with the cancel button.

If you run the app now, you should be able to use either button to dismiss the modal – if it works, well done, that's what you were looking to achieve by this stage. However, we're not done yet; we now want to be able to add a task to a list and then fresh from table View so the new task shows up.

We need a central place for all these tasks. You also need a really good definition of a task so, let's put the Save feature to one side and get to work on those bits first.

Our Core Business Objects

It is important that your core business objectives are modeled separately from your user interface because it makes them more flexible and gives them a portability, which you would need if you ever decided to make your app work on other platforms. It doesn't take much to do it, just a Task struct and a TaskStore class.

Creating the Task Struct

Open File>New>File or use Cmd+N to create a new file. This time though you do not want a Cocoa Touch Class, simply a Swift file. Call the file Task (.swift gets put on automatically) and then you need to create the Task struct in the file:

- struct Task {
- let title: String
- let notes: String
- init(title: String, notes: String) {
- self.title = title
- self.notes = notes
- }
- }

Now, you have probably realized already that there isn't any way to edit the task and that is correct. Instead, we are going to take the functional style that Swift is aimed at and create an immutable value object. What that means is, when you need to make a change to a task, you will simply get rid of the old one and pence it with a brand new task. Your users will see it as having been edited but your aim is to make life easier for you as a developer by creating less mutable state.

Managing Our Taskstore

Now we need another Swift file for the TaskStore. This is going to be set up as a singleton so that you can access the one instance whenever you want, both adding and editing tasks as you wish. Create a file in the same way as you did for Task.swift but, this time, call it TaskStore:

- class TaskStore {

- class var sharedInstance: TaskStore {

- struct Static {

- static let instance = TaskStore()

- }

- return Static.instance

- }

- var tasks: [Task] = []

- func add(task: Task) {

- tasks.append(task)

- }

- func replace(task: Task, atIndex index: Int) {

- tasks[index] = task

- }

- func get(index: Int) -> Task {

- return tasks[index]

- }

- }

The first few lines of this TaskStore class give you a way to use a singleton version of the taskStore, which can be accessed with TaskStore.saredInstance.

Then you have a number of basic functions - Add, Replace, Get tasks from the list. You can replace this in the future with something a little more suitable but this will suite out purpose for now.

Finishing Our First Feature

As a little test, I'd like you to have a go at finishing off the Save feature that we started earlier. You don't need to worry about displaying the task list, we'll cover that shortly. I'll give you a clue as to how to complete it – Name the segue from the Save button and make sure you use the prepareForSegue:sender method.

Part 3 – Finishing off

So, how did you do with the task of finishing off Save? Your code should look something like this:

- if segue.identifier == "dismissAndSave" {

- let task = Task(title: titleField.text, notes: notesField.text)

- TaskStore.sharedInstance.add(task)

- }

Of course, you also need to ensure that you have all the correct identifiers for every segue in the Storyboard. If you didn't manage to complete it, here's how:

Once again, open up Main.Storyboard and complete the segues from the buttons to AddTaskViewController and MasterViewController; make sure they have relevant names such as DismissandSave and DismissandCancel. This makes it nice and easy to identify them.

In the AddTaskViewController.swift file, we are going to set up the prepareForSegue:sender method we talked about earlier.

- override func prepareForSegue(segue: UIStoryboardSegue, sender: AnyObject!) {

- if segue.identifier == "dismissAndSave" {

- let task = Task(title: titleField.text, notes: notesField.text)

- TaskStore.sharedInstance.add(task)

- }

- }

First you must check that you are preparing this for the right segue – it should be the Save segue because the Cancel segue is going to do everything it should do anyway – precisely nothing!

Even when you have just one segue to set up, it is good practice to be explicit about the name of the segue you are running the code for. That way, if things change later on, the developer, in this case, you know exactly how everything is connected and what bit goes where.

Once you have identified your segue, you are now going to give a constant a new task – filling out the task from the text fields. After that, you can use TaskStore to look after your Task by adding it to sharedInstance.

Try running the application now – it should all work just fine until you get to the List, at which point it will just stop. There should not be any crashes and things should run fairly smoothly. However, there really is little point in saving a task if you can't see it so let's move on to the next feature.

Listing Tasks

Before we start to customize too much, let's see how far you can get with what you already have. When we first generated this project, we had a MasterViewController that had the basic data source and delegate methods already set up, and that included deletion. We also had a very basic DetailViewContoller.

Start by opening up the MasterViewController.swift file and let's make a few changes. First, we want to get rid of the unwanted objects property so go to the top of the file and delete the line that looks like:

- var objects = NSMutableArray()

We no longer need that now but removing it is going to upset Xcode because that very same property is used in a number of places. Fix the errors in order, from top to bottom, replacing old code with the new TaskStore code.

Opening the Detail Screen

The first place you will see an error is in the prepareForSegue:sender: method of the MasterViewController. We need to change two lines of the if statement:

- override func prepareForSegue(segue: UIStoryboardSegue, sender: AnyObject?) {

- if segue.identifier == "showDetail" {

- ifletindexPath=self.tableView.indexPathForSelectedRow()
  {

- let task = TaskStore.sharedInstance.get(indexPath.row)

- (segue.destinationViewController   as
  DetailViewController).detailItem = task

- }

- }

- }

On line 2 inside the if statement, change the constant name from Object to task and, in the sharedInstance of the TaskStore, use the Get method to get the task you want.

On the third line inside the if statement, change the detailItem of the DetailviewController from object to Task – this is only because you have changed the Constant name.

The next problem to fix is inside the DetailViewController so open up the .swift file to make a change – right now, that articular view controller is expecting an AnyObject? And this means that the struct we made earlier isn't going to fit in. So, we fix that by changing the detailedItem type to be Task? instead:

- var detailItem: Task? {

- didSet {

- // Update the view.

- self.configureView()

- }

- }

While you are in here, you may as well fix the rest of the problems. It won't take a lot; you just need to change the method of the configureView. Unwrapping the detailItem optional, you see that it is of AnyObject type, which we now know, isn't true because we just changed it. And, Task doesn't have any description property so we can change that to title:

- func configureView() {

- // Update the user interface for the detail item.

- if let detail: Task = self.detailItem {

- if let label = self.detailDescriptionLabel {

- label.text = detail.title

- }

- }

- }

That's it, that's all you need to change in the DetailViewController until design changes start appearing so we can now go back to MasterViewController.Swift and finish fixing that.

Changing the Data Source and Delegate

The next error to fix is UITableViewDataSource protocol method:

- tableView:numberOfRowsInSection:

Right now, you are calling cont. on what used to be an array of

APPS

objects. Instead we want to call count on the SharedInstance of TaskStore:

- override func tableView(tableView: UITableView, numberOfRowsInSection section: Int) -> Int {

- return TaskStore.sharedInstance.count

- }

Of course, at the moment, you do not actually have a count property so we'll create that right now. Open the taskStore.swift file and, under the Tasks property declaration, adding this:

- var count: Int {

- get {

- return tasks.count

- }

- }

You could have created a method like this as well:

- func count() -> Int {

- return tasks.count

- }

It's shorter but it certainly lacks the style of the first method though. By creating count as a computed property, you are able to keep a consistent API with Array and are not essentially forcing a property into a method.

What you may not know at this moment is that we can make this even more concise. Computed properties have no setter so you can remove the second and fourth lines and have it read like this instead:

- var count: Int {

- return tasks.count

- }

Back to the Data Source

Putting aside all the small but nice things we can do with Swift, it's time to finish the data source. Let's move on to the tableView:cel lForRowAtIndexPath: method. The change in this one is similar to the prepareForSegue:sender: method change. All we are doing is changing how we get the Task and from which property we are using it from:

- override func tableView(tableView: UITableView, cellForRowAtIndexPath indexPath: NSIndexPath) -> UITableViewCell {

- let cell = tableView.dequeueReusableCellWithIdentifier("C ell", forIndexPath: indexPath) as UITableViewCell

- let task = TaskStore.sharedInstance.get(indexPath.row)

- cell.textLabel?. text = task.title

- return cell

- }

The two lines we changed here are the two that are just before the Return statement. We are changing the Objects array and the subscript operator for the Get method from the TaskStore, assigning the result to the Task constant ahead of Object. On the last line before the statement, we have changed the text property of the textLabel to the name of the task you have got.

There is only one thing left to change and that is one of the delegate methods.

You can probably already see that you have an error left to fix, in the UITableViewDelegate method: tableView:commitEditingStyle :forRowAtIndexPath:

The change is simple but you are going to need to add to your TaskStore again:

- override func tableView(tableView: UITableView, commitEditingStyle editingStyle: UITableViewCellEditingStyle, forRowAtIndexPath indexPath: NSIndexPath) {

- if editingStyle == .Delete {

- TaskStore.sharedInstance.removeTaskAtIndex(indexPath.row)

- tableView.deleteRowsAtIndexPaths([indexPath], withRowAnimation: .Fade)

- } else if editingStyle == .Insert {

- // Create a new instance of the appropriate class, insert it into the array, and add a new row to the table view.

- }

- }

We only needed to change one line here:

- objects.removeObjectAtIndex(indexPath.row), changed to

- TaskStore.sharedInstance.removeTaskAtIndex(indexPath. row) inside Delete part of the if statement

This method doesn't exist just yet, so we need to create that now.

Open TaskStore.Swift and add in the following at the end:

- func removeTaskAtIndex(index: Int) {

- tasks.removeAtIndex(index)

- }

The reason we did it this way, instead of directly accessing tasks array is that it lets you define an API for the consumers of the TaskStore class. Later, you will be able to change the internals for this without breaking up any other code in the process.

What you can do if you want to is make a couple of changes to the design to enhance your application. First of all open Main. Storyboard and click on the prototype table view and now we are going to change the style from the default UITableViewStyle to the subtitle style. One you have selected the table, you can change the style in the Attributes Inspector. The new subtitle provides you with a second text label.

With that, we are going to make a few changes to the MasterViewController to take advantage of that extra label. Open up MasterViewController.Swift and locate the tableView:cellForR owAtIndexPath: method. Make the following changes:

- override func tableView(tableView: UITableView, cellForRowAtIndexPath indexPath: NSIndexPath) -> UITableViewCell {

- let cell = tableView.dequeueReusableCellWithIdentifier("C ell", forIndexPath: indexPath) as UITableViewCellre

- let task = TaskStore.sharedInstance.get(indexPath.row)

- cell.textLabel?.text = task.title

- cell.detailTextLabel?.text = task.notes

- return cell

- }

The only real change we are making is that we are setting the text property of the detailTextLabel. Now when you run the application, if you add a task and fill out the notes field, a preview of your notes shows up when the task list comes up. The next thing we are going to change is what happens when you fill out the text field with too many characters.

Redesigning the Detail View

The small label in the center isn't really enough so open Main. Storyboard so we can make some changes to DetailViewController. It doesn't matter here what you make this look like, but for now, just follow this example. The first is already in DetailViewController so just rag the label up to the top and enlarge the size a little. Don't forget to update the constraints.

Now go into the Object Library and drag a Text View out. Go into the Attributes Inspector and let's play about with the layout. First, change the font to 18 points – remember you can get into the font picker by clicking the T in the font field. Next, uncheck the box beside Editable, just under the font field. Now check the boxes beside Links and Phone numbers – you will find those in the Detection section. Lastly, link the DetailViewController and the Text View. Open the Assistant Editor, hold CTRL and drag from the Text View to just beneath the definition of @IBOutlet. Call the new outlets notesView.

Now that you have created the outlet, the only thing left to do is put some content into it. Open DetailViewController.swift, locate the configureView file and make these changes:

- func configureView() {

- // Update the user interface for the detail item.

- if let detail: Task = self.detailItem {

- if let label = self.detailDescriptionLabel {

- label.text = detail.title

- }

- }

- }

You can see what we've done – look inside the new if statement that is inside the wrapping if statement. Another thing we have done is removed "self" from the beginning of all the properties.

All that remains to be said now is congratulations on completing your very first iOS app in Swift!

CHAPTER 9

Do's and Don'ts of App Development

In the last few years, more than a million apps have been built by thousands of developers and that number is growing by the day. Developers have already earned in excess of $8 billion from the iOS app store alone, without taking into account the other mobile platforms. But success is something of an illusion as the small developers are struggling to get a foothold in a market dominated by the big players with the big money. Out of the top 250 publishers in the iOS app store, only 2% of them are newcomers so, for those who are looking to be the next big thing in mobile app development, here are some tips for you from the experts:

DO

Scale Your Idea Down to Something That is Really Useful

Think about what you are building – if it isn't an app that people are likely to use several times a day, don't bother building it. Take a tip from Loren Bricter. He built an app called Tweetie, which is a hugely popular Twitter Inc app that Twitter themselves eventually purchased. He said that probably discards around 80% of his ideas and keeps his focus on those that are sticky. For example, there is a good reason why some of the biggest apps out there include photo-sharing services – taking photos is one of the biggest uses of the mobile phone.

Learn Some of the Fundamentals of Coding

You do not need to be a technical wizard to build apps these days. Apple gives you all the tools you need to help you develop your app but you should still have a basic understanding of the coding. This will help you to be a little wiser when it comes to building your app so that you don't produce something that uses up all the resources and battery on a user's mobile.

Include Features That Will Interest a User

If you really want to irritate your mobile app users, build in a static screen that does nothing. Users like things to be happening all the time in their apps so incorporate a few progress bars or animations that keep their attention focused while they wait for things to load up

Test Your App Wisely

Whereas you can tweak a desktop website as you go, you can't do that with a mobile one. So, make sure you use the right people to test your apps out before you launch them on an unsuspecting public.

Cross Promote

Building the app is only half of it; you have to work hard at promoting it as well. Try to cross promote it with other apps – when you run your other apps, include a small banner or icon that users can tap to be taken to your new app.

DON'T

Stick With a Single Business Model

The days where developers need to choose between developing a paid app or a free app are over and most are incorporating the two together these days. Some make free apps that have in-app purchases while others charge a small amount for the app and then charge for premium features.

Once other thing you can consider doing is charging for your app but, every now and again, giving it away for free, just for a short period. That can jump-start downloads of the app and, if you cross promote another app within that app, you'll pick up even more revenue.

Get Stuck Using One-Atop Development Platforms

One of the biggest headaches that mobile app developers face today is in building their apps to suit more than one platform. There are some technologies that are trying to ease the burden and offer up a one-stop platform that allows you to develop your app for several different systems. While those can save quite a bit of time and money, they are also very compromising. You end up with an app that is nothing special because you lose many of the special features along the way. Although it is time consuming, you are better off building your app for each platform individually.

Copy Other Ideas

If you can't come up with something unique, don't waste your time. There are already way too many photo apps, for example. Look at each product category in your chosen app store and see just what's available and, perhaps more importantly, what isn't before you get down to the business of building your app.

Update Your App Too Frequently

Once your app is launched, it is inevitable that there will need to be bug fixes and pates and there is no rule how long you should wait between versions. The experts suggest that you wait until you have a genuine new feature before you update, rather than fixing every single little problem as it happens.

Build a Mobile App when You Can Easily Build a Website

Just because mobile apps are the current big thing, it doesn't mean that they are suitable for you. If you have a lot of content that you want to get across, a website is the better option. You can then build a mobile version of the website, rather than going through all the pain of developing a mobile app that isn't going to work properly.

Interesting facts About Mobile Phones and Apps

Most people have a mobile phone of some description these days and 90% of them are smartphones. Are you having a hard time convincing yourself or your boss that you need a mobile app? Take a look at these figures and see if they convince you:

1. Almost 60% of US consumers who are aged 16 or over own at least one smartphone each.

2. The US 16 and over market is the second largest technology market in the world, following China

3. In the last 3 years, the number of people who browse the internet and use social networking sites via a mobile device has risen significantly, shooting past the 1.2 billion mark.

4. Mobile internet traffic accounts for nearly 20% of all internet traffic in the world

5. Mobile devices using the existing diagonal screen configuration occupy no more than 20% of all mobile device sales in the world, meaning that the huge variety of mobile devices is expanding by the day.

6. More than 60% of online shoppers use their smartphones while in a grocery store or supermarket and a 50% use them on the way to the store

7. 90% of mobile device owners admit to switching between different devices to get a job completed. Devices are listed as smartphones, tablets, desktop PC, Mac, laptop, even Smart TV's.

8. By the end of this year there will be nearly 1 billion internet tablets in circulation

9. 85% of emails are read on a mobile phone and 16% on a tablet

10. Mobile search engines are responsible for more than 25% of all internet search queries

11. 95% of all smartphone owners user their devices to search for brand information

12. Mobile device owners spend more than 50% more on their devices than they do on buying a new PC.

And Finally – Fun Mobile Facts

- The very first mobile phone call was made in St Louis, Missouri. It was made from a car on June 17th 1946 using Bell System's Mobile Telephone Service.

- The mobile app economy is responsible for the creation of more than half a million jobs in the US alone

- The very first smartphone was not the iPhone, although there are those who stick to that like glue! In fact, it was an IBM Simon Personal Communicator from COMDEX and it was announced in November 1992. It was a huge device with a stylus for touch input, a choice of 1 or 1.8 MB memory, and a large nickel-cadmium battery that gave around 1 hour of talk time. It had a price tag of $599 and is now a true collector's item.

- The very first SMS message was sent on December 3 1992. It went from a computer to a mobile device and was sent in the UK by Neil Papworth to his friend Richard Jarvis; the message said "Merry Christmas".

- The word "smartphone" did not come into existence until 1997. It came from Erickson when they described their GS 88 "Penelope" concept as a smart phone.

- The most expensive smartphone in the world was claimed to have been created by Stuart Hughes, a British jeweler. It was an iPhone 4 and it came with the name Diamond Rose. It has a price tag of £5 million and has a bezel made of rose gold and decorated with more than 500 flawless diamonds, totaling more than 100 carats. The back of the phone is rose gold and has a rose gold apple logo with 53 diamonds. Since then, every subsequent iPhone, and other manufacturers models, have been given the same treatment

- The very first mobile phone appeared in 1973, made by martin Cooper of Motorola. It was called the DynaTAC 8000X and was released commercially in 1984. At the time, it cost $3995, which today equates to about $9000. It weighed in at a hefty 2.5 lbs. and the first call was made by Cooper to his nearest rival.

- In the last 12-15 years, the numbers of people taking out mobile phone subscriptions has rocketed to more than 6 billion.

APPS

- Fear of losing your mobile phone has its own name – Nomophobia. It is a phobia that at least half of the world population suffers from.

- Did you know that it takes upwards of 26 hours for a person to report that their wallet or purse is missing? It takes just 68 minutes for people to report their smartphone missing.

Conclusion

Thank you again for downloading this book!

I hope this book was able to provide you with guidance in entering the field of mobile app development.

Mobile app development can be really profitable but it requires time and effort. This guide is just the beginning. As you gain experience in app development, you'll learn lessons that no book can give you. Nonetheless, this book can help you get started on the right note.

Now, the next step for you is to start creating your own apps. Always remember that quality is the key. You can advertise and promote your app as much as you like but it won't do well if it's not inherently good. The development of your app is a continuous process and does not end when you publish it. Use multiple sources for your learning and make your app as valuable as possible to your users.

Don't stop learning. The mobile app development field is constantly changing at a rate faster than we would like. Keep yourself updated since what works now might become obsolete in a matter of days.

Free Bonus Video: Engineering an Android App: How to Design, Build and Test

Here is an extra video that goes more into depth with a tutorial on how build an android app.

Bonus Video: https://www.youtube.com/watch?v=E8BVJWcEqHE

Checkout My Other Books

- **http://www.amazon.com/Hacking-Basic-Security-Penetration-Testing-ebook/dp/B00VC70PGY/ref=sr_1_5?s=digital-text&ie=UTF8&qid=1430258156&sr=1-5&keywords=hacking**

CPSIA information can be obtained
at www.ICGtesting.com
Printed in the USA
LVHW011756181119
637700LV00013B/1723/P

9 781511 988698